Travelling Mercies

BOOKS BY LORNA GOODISON

POETRY
Tamarind Season
I Am Becoming My Mother
Heartease
Selected Poems
To Us, All Flowers Are Roses
Turn Thanks
Guinea Woman: New and Selected Poems
Travelling Mercies

FICTION
Baby Mother and the King of Swords

Travelling Mercies

LORNA GOODISON

National Library of Canada Cataloguing in Publication Data

Goodison, Lorna
Travelling mercies

Poems.
ISBN 0-7710-3382-6

1. Caribbean Area – Poetry. 2. Jamaica – Poetry. I. Title.

PS8563.083435T72ʹ 2001   C811ʹ.54   C00-933033-X
PR9199.3.G66T72 2001

We acknowledge the financial support of the Government of Canada
through the Book Publishing Industry Development Program for
our publishing activities. We further acknowledge the support of
the Canada Council for the Arts and the Ontario Arts Council for our
publishing program.

The epigraph on page 55 is from the play *Joe Turner's Come and Gone* by
August Wilson. Copyright © 1988 by August Wilson. Used by permission
of Dutton Signet, a division of Penguin Putnam Inc.

Typeset in Garamond by M&S, Toronto
Printed and bound in Canada

McClelland & Stewart Ltd.
The Canadian Publishers
481 University Avenue
Toronto, Ontario
M5G 2E9
www.mcclelland.com

1   2   3   4   5   05   04   03   02   01

For John Edward

CONTENTS

SPENDING THE GOLD OF LOVERS

Pearl morning, when the Blue Mountains
contracted and stamped themselves, imprimatur,
across your forehead. You witnessed the seal
in the mirror as you combed your hair.

By sun hot, words began to issue from your lips,
words for which you had no meaning like "Lailah"
which means "a night," and "Ali" who later became
your rose seller.

Like dusk, the rain of coins fell, downpouring
from vents in the ceiling. Gold you gather
and spend freehand, careless and wanton
in your sojournings.

Come winter, a wine-bibber on the number 5 bus
is inviting anyone who so desires to dine with him.
"Anyone who wants to can come, I have money,
I can pay."

The same gold rain was falling down,
leaking out from the vault of his rented room,
lining his pockets so he became profligate
deaf to the warnings

of the saved and reasonable woman cautioning
"put away that money for rainy days."
"No," he maintained, "I can pay, I will pay,
and whosoever will may come."

TRAVELLING MERCIES

are what we petition
as we row in rough barks
walk foot, or wing

in silver gaulins.
Approaching Castries,
send travelling mercies.

Call them down
for anxious traveller
homing to old mother

herself travelling
in small Morne room
en route to mansions.

Sanction this request
and swift send
journey mercies.

And you, away
from new husband,
brood over Caribbean,

keep us on this voyage
to union,
send down travelling mercies.

WHAT WE CARRIED THAT CARRIED US

I

SONG AND STORY

In ship's belly, song and story dispensed as medicine,
story and song, bay rum and camphor for faint way.

Song propelled you to fly through hidden other eye,
between seen eyes and out of structure, hover.

In barks of destruction, story functioned as talisman
against give-up death, cramped paralysed darkness.

Remaining remnant tasting all of life, blood, salt,
bitter wet sugar. Ball of light, balance power,

pellucid spirit wafer without weight, ingested,
taken in as nourishment, leaven within the system.

Remnant remaining rise now.

II

DANCE ROCKSTEADY

You danced upon the deck of the slaver *Antonia*
named for the cherubic daughter of sea captain Fraser.
Aye kumina.

4

You moved just so, in and out between wild notes
sounded by the suicide followers, staying well within
rock steady rhythm,

range of Kilimanjaro, length of river Limpopo.
Respond again to higher rimshot and one drop
ride rocksteady.

The living converter woman of Green Island
sings in morning as she passes through the valley
"Farewell Night Angel." She's on her way to the butcher shop,

all the verdant valley ringing
with coloratura converter singing.

Last week she received revelation as she bent over
the tinnin bucket, turning intestines inside out,
shedding the green grass waste of the cow and the goat.

She has turned at least twenty million feet
of tripe on the sceptre of her tripe stick.

Tripe is not straight so. Like all to do with history
long story and memory, it is coiled and sectioned.
Here the uneatable bitter tubing, roped conduit of gall,

here the gold-celled honeycomb,
and within all the leaved book

recording abominable drama in ship's maw
tragedy of captured and capturer

scenes that seemed to be calling
for overdue acts of conversion.

So the Converter sing

comfort, console, people sold out
dark flesh cargo

drogued in beast state
in the name of cane profit.

Sound myrrh notes to quell
putrefaction's smell.

Cleanse the charnel house
of the bloodbath Atlantic.

Chant new baptismals
for the ones of lost names,

digging song and burial song
for whip, rack, gibbet and chain.

Raise outlaw anthems
to lionheart fight-back.

Coo of the compassion
of Abolition's barbary doves.

Line and sight gratitude psalms,
recite names of resisters,

hoist high notes as guidons
to tramplers of banners of blood.

Divine and cause compunction
skywater to fall.

Scatter grudge clouds
seeding bullet storms.

Hum down vengeance,
call for response reparations.

Summon the wordsmiths,
dancers and artists

singers and players
of instruments must be there.

Honest merchants who follow
the profession of the Prophet.

Blessed be the sowers
and apostles who catch fish.

High Holy ones all charged
to restore legacy of wisdom,

true word ancient
time come, must be fulfilled.

Then balm and anoint
the heads of the young

to call forth and bring in
as yet unknown

fresh revelation and
new moon's understanding.

Even so, is so
the Converter did sing.

NEVER EXPECT

Burchell the Baptist
handed you the landpapers.
You were not in a position
to read them, so you call
the name of your place
into the responding wind

by so doing recreating
your ancestral ceremony
of naming. "Never Expect"
you name your place,
your own spot to cultivate
a small start-over Eden.

Plot for fruit and flowering trees
for your children.
Burying ground for family tombs
and navel strings.
Your strict drawn boundary line
against intruder,

prickle dildo-makka fence
militant as living barbwire.
Begin with one room, piecen it,
fling open your door
or turn your key
when you private.

Build your firewall high.
Raise up your wide barbecue.
Pop loud laugh for peasoup.
Remark openly upon
your ceiling of the sky
and its shifting shade of blue.

Hosanna you build your house.
Yes, Alleluia, you never expect it.

> *If Quashee will not honestly aid in bringing-out those*
> *sugars, cinnamons and nobler products of the West-*
> *Indian Islands, for the benefit of all mankind, then I say*
> *neither will the Powers permit Quashee to continue*
> *growing pumpkins there for his own lazy benefit . . .*
> *Not a pumpkin, Quashee, not a square yard of soil.*
> — Thomas Carlyle, *The Nigger Question*

It was bad magic made with pen and ink.
Follow-line soldier-crab hieroglyphics
show off drop-hand scatter mark

employed by Thomas Carlyle to ask
the Nigger Question: Can England afford
to give pumpkin-eating Quashie freedom?

Bookless Quashie had no opportunity
to make said Carlyle guess and spell
how water find way into pumpkin belly.

Freedom comes, Quashie receives nothing
but desires own book to open and sight
read and interpret, revise and analyse.

So beginning from a position of zero
Quashie gathers sundry different papers
that have writing, words and picture.

Part of that letter from Queen Victoria
advising Q to save, and study thrift.
Obscene handbills advertising Q for sale.

Refuses to include verse five Ephesians six
or the hymn of rich man in his castle
poor man at his gate, God made them

every one and ordered their estate.
Q wishes to hear no more about estate.
But includes four bills of lading for cloth

for downpresser, from raw silk to bombazine.
And the paper that claimed that Queen Victoria
has given Quashie, as of first of August, full free.

All this was assembled, impaled and jooked
upon a long spike pointed like Q's story.
And yea verily, that was our first book.

ABOUT THE TAMARIND

Under strict dry conditions I can grow as high
as eighty feet, and my open frame half as wide.
Then my trunk which yields a kind of timber
called by some the mahogany of Madeira
will become too substantial and stout for you
to wrap your short arms around.

My crown, a mass of fine light green foliage,
pinnate leaves which dip gracefully to shade you
fold in upon themselves at night, private.
I bloom small gold flowers which appear
to bleed the gold of guinea and the blood
drawn by the cut of slavery.

I am slow growing, rooted deep, resisting
breeze blow, hot air and hurricane winds.
I flourish even in rocky terrain with little or no
cultural attention. My suede brown pods
grow in profusion. I bear long, I bear abundance
and Pharaohs ate of me.

Tamr-hindi, the Persian poet chanted under my shade.
Rooted first in Africa, transplanted wherever
I can thrive, that is wherever there is sun of life,
I require his constant kiss in order to flourish.
His hot caresses I absorb and return in the form
of fire purifying, all-consuming.

Tamarindus indica, native of Africa, from root
to leaftip my every part has been employed
to meet human need. Consider how they eat
my flowers and leaves, roast my seeds, pound them
into paste for sizing. My fruit, which is sometimes sour,
can be sugared into tamarind balls, symbols of slavery.

Sometimes in alluvial soil I grow large and sweet,
that is in places where I am valued and needed.
Then I heal. Refrigerant for fevers, I am laxative.
I work alone or can combine with juice of limes
or extrusion of bees. Together we can cure
bilious digestive systems large as those of elephants.

I reduce swellings, loosen the grip of paralysis
and return the drunken inebriated on illusion,
the cheap coarse wine of the world, to sobriety,
perhaps to become one day truly drunk like me
with Khayyam's wine unseen which causes me to sway
so that the unanointed mock me.

In Africa they soak my bark with corn
and feed this to domestic birds in the belief
that if they stray or are stolen they will return.
In Asia, a nectar of tamarind and coconut milk
is touched to the lips of infants as their first drink,
the world's initial welcoming libation.

And the elephant's long memory is aided by the eating
of my bark and the pods, flesh and seeds of my fruit.

My leaves give soothing bush baths for rashes or the cut
of the tamarind whip. The correction and the cure
both come from me. There are believers who claim
I am dwelling place of the spirit of rain.

I raise the temperature in my immediate vicinity
so the cold-hearted fear me. I will tell you now why
few plants grow wild beneath me, and why you
should not use me as policetree to tether your horse
because I have not come to rule over, overpower,
vanquish, conquer or constrain anyone.

I provide the mordant in dyes. Burn me for charcoal,
I rise as incense. My sapwood is pale and golden.
My heartwood, though, is royal purple and earth brown.
I am high and low all at once. Sour and sweet,
I came with the enslaved across the seas to bear for you
when force-ripe capricious crops fail.

I bear. Not even the salt of the ocean can stunt me.
Plant me on abiding rock or foaming restless waters.
Set me in burying grounds, I grow shade for ancestors.
O bitter weed and dry-heart tree, wait for me to bow.
I hope you can wait. Rest in Peace, Arawaks.
I am still here, still bearing after five hundred years.

WAS IT LEGBA SHE MET OUTSIDE THE CORONATION MARKET?

Under the arch of the Coronation Market
she watches the crooked man approach,
he is a dromedary with a double hump,
one of muscle and cartilage, one a crocus bag sack
swollen with the rank weeds and fragrant leaves
of his travelling bush doctor's business.

He bends over and over-looks the child.
She can see the red-veined whites of his eyes,
he leans backward and then falls into a trance
during which he removes his eye's white ball
and swallows it. It reappears in her palm. She returns
the white sphere, he swallows it and speaks prophecy.

Then he limps away with his halt legba walk
but she is left at the crossroads hearing the call,
spirits assembled, casting their lots to decide
who will claim her voice and speak through it
the as yet untold half. Her mother returns, laden down
with ground provisions. The child is silent as the ball's
white weight levitates on the tip of her tongue.

That Kingston's dungle is called "Moonlight City"
and Lupus can assume the mask of a butterfly,
that Judas found it necessary to kiss Jesus
is that obstinate beauty's apology for what is vile?

You want eagle's mastery do you bribe D Lawrence
and hitch a broom ride. You see seamstresses living
on pensions earned from stitching up the wounds
you inflicted on the world with your long knives

so you turn and sue your neighbour over property
that is not your own in order to win and spend
what is Caesar's and enter into what you despise –
back door dealings, choke and rob and easy life.

Behold now the peerless flush shade of crimson
blood drawn, mellifluous the betrayer's voice
as he baits you up with gossip hook and line.
But beauty bids you cleanly contemplate the folly

of it all. Discern the shafts of light pointing from
betrayer's knife to blind spirit murderer at his task.
For then he might be led eyeless to gaze
inside, thereby to understand how a landfill

can be called moonlight city, how Iscariot
was must and bound to kiss his friend Christ.
And why Lupus, the wasting spawn of wolves,
can assume the winged mask of butterflies.

RUN GREYHOUND

April dawns in the Ann Arbor Greyhound bus terminal,
a lithe girl tells a man with the locks of a gorgon

how she set out after Jack Kerouac to write a road novel
but her car and craft stalled by the Grand Ole Opry

so she boarded a bus to this station and is awaiting
the coming of her mother who will pilot her home.

He allows as how he has done his travelling in the grape
vineyards of California and the peach groves of Georgia

where he tangled with the law, and ninety days later
"behold, a new man" declares the free-standing gorgon.

Lithe girl presses throat hard to free response, but timely
timely and fortuitously her good mother comes,

blessed turnkey securing prodigal daughter's release.
In unison they refuse offers of help from locked penitent.

Fifteen minutes behind time the silver Greyhound runs in,
gorgon-locks boards with his belongings in a trash bag.

"All these men were released from prison this morning"
whispers a woman accompanying a man with an eye patch.

Riding into the city of Detroit on the convict bus
let the muster now record: one man with a red bandana

muttering steady urgent encouragement to greyhound
to make up the lost fifteen minutes of missing time;

the twin of a bankrupt country and western singer
crooning "fifteen years, fifteen years of my life

I'm sick and tired of being sick and tired of myself";
whispering woman, "become your own best friend";

a man, thick cigar store Indian, knuckles of one hand
forming bone buckle at the waist of his pants, says

"imagine I'm the one to make restitution in the sum
of a thousand dollars and attend a turnaround program";

two silent black men in new clothes and Nikes
whom the driver orders to disembark at Wayne.

The bus pulled into their stop. They sat. They did not get up.
The man with the eye patch clutches an x-ray of his head.

The woman beside him insists on whispering. You begin
to make strong supplication along with man in bandana,

for eye-patch is beginning to look like Henry Morgan,
retired wicked buccaneer and born-again governor,

the driver like J Edgar Hoover, the others like Tippu Tip,
Augusto Pinochet, Margaret Thatcher, Émile Zola,

the blood of Cézanne curdling on the nib of his pen.
You make supplication to the swift chariot to run,

you intone "run greyhound run" as we pass through Indian
    country
deer fields, where Tecumseh will take us for the long-knife
    cavalry.

Run greyhound

for leaking caravelles of discovery are upon us, and some
still have just bamboo arrows tipped with cuttlefish bones

and others have mad dogs and fouling pieces, sheep cloning
pox blankets, anthrax warfare, agent orange, blunderbusses.

Go greyhound

press driver press, pedal to the metal to the motor city.
Make up for time lost this day, fifteen minutes, ninety days,

five hundred Babylonian years.

Run, hound of the Pharaohs, run like the twinned Blue Nile
to meet your white same-source branch at Khartoum.

To the city of Detroit where patients discharged from a state
mental hospital clutch sour pillows and wait to take these seats,

where a woman arrayed in scarlet lamé chain mail
with a wighat, hirsute visor, overhanging her brow

is slashing out let-live and mercy and forgiveness
where they appear in the text of a creased Bible tract

and two latchkey children lock hands and pipe reed-like
about the impossibility of being separated from their dignity.

In silver tones how they flute, they coo, baby Barbary doves.
Run greyhound run, for they are waiting to board this bus.

And so we proceeded along the built-up mud banking
above a water course like an infernal Bog Walk gorge
with fog draped like wet sheets against fire burning.
Just as how people in foreign build thick mud walls
to keep out big sea when it rises up high and swells
to overflow their food cultivations and pasture lands
in places like British and French Guyana near Brazil.
Or some Italian town named Padua along the Brent
where they erect big retaining walls with weep-holes
to protect tower and yard against deconstruction's
snowmelt, earthrunnings, carrydown and watershed.
It's as if hell's civil engineer got an illegal gully contract
to bitch-up some similar but lean-side walls like that.
By now we are travelling in the bowels of the earth
leaving the murdersuicide woodland so far out of sight
we could not spy it even from the land of look behind.
We buck up a procession of duppies shuffling below
the banking, staring up into our faces like how some
scrutinize one another under the light of a new moon.
Staring, like fast people trying to see who passing by
dark road on a moonless night; staring, like an old tailor
with glaucoma trying hard to thread a fine-eyed needle.
The staring duppies screwed their faces and frowned,
then one sight me, grab me by the hem of my gown
and said, "Lord have mercy, could this really be true.
Dear poet is it you?" As he touched me I focused hard
riveting my eyes upon the charred skin of his face

so that I summoned up his image from my memory.
And bending near, I peered into his burnt countenance
and groaned, "Is it you down here so Teacher Brown?"
"O my friend I do hope you will not object if Brownman
turns around and walks along by your side so allowing
this ghostly procession to proceed a while without me."
Said I, "I would be most honoured if you and I could sit in,
if it pleases him who is my guide through this dark pit."
Said Mr. B., "Whichever one of this done-dead-already band
stops for a moment must remain still for a hundred years,
forbidden to brush off these drops of corrosive acid rain.
No, my good friend, do walk on, I will walk below you
until it will be time for me to rejoin my duppy company
who must perpetually weep and wail in eternal flames."
So since I dared not descend from my banking and walk
with him on the burning no-life path, I inclined my head,
walked with it bowed low to show my respect, like a mystic
meditating reverently upon the divide between goodness
and evil. "And what brings you down here before your time?
Was it that big accident up by Providence? And who is he
that is leading you through this dive of such deep darkness?"
Hear me: "Up there in the land of the living, I went astray,
I lost my livity, lost my way before I reached the fullness
of my years, only yesterday before day did I find myself
and this master here appeared and wheel and turned me
like a Revivalist Darwish/Sufi and is now leading me home."
Hear him: "Follow your guiding star, for in all the good life
I experienced I learned this one thing that's true. What is fi
you, can not be un-fi you. And had I lived out my time
and purpose, instead of having it cut short, I would have

helped, supported and encouraged your work, seeing that
you are a true poet, God-blessed. But that bad-minded set,
those pharisaical keepers of our country's gates, whose
hearts are as hard as Blue Mountain alabaster, those who
occupy the chairs of the colonial masters, they envy you
your talent. But poet, the roseapple was not ever meant
to flourish beside these blighted soursop trees, bear in mind
that even old proverbs call them blind-guides, a bad mind
petty, mean spirited, myopic kind; take care to uproot
their grudging ways from your heart. It is written in the stars.
It must surely come to pass that your honours will make
both parties want to claim you. That ram goat will never
reach high enough to crop on such sweet grass, let them
devour their one another's (excuse me) one another's rass.
But never let them cut down any innocent plant that
despite their stunting hands will still thrive amongst them."
"Mr. Brown, if I had my wish," I said, "you wouldn't be
banished from the land of the living in which you were
a source of light among our people. I recall your gentle
compassionate and fatherly face as you taught me daily
how human beings can make themselves live eternally.
This image of you, pentimento, surfaces on my heart and
lives on in my mind and while I am alive I give thanks
for it, and I will tell of you to the world through my life
and my art. Your predictions for my future I will file
with some works of mine I save to show a wise someone
who will be the judge of these matters anon, if I can ever
reach her higherheights. As the Most High is my witness
I tell you this: As long as, I say, as long as my conscience
is clear, I am prepared for whatever destiny shall bring

my way. Twice already, I have heard that same prophecy.
But let Fortune's wheel turn around as it pleases, round
and round she must go and countryman must dig with hoe."
My spirit guide paused when he heard what it was I said,
turned and looked into my eyes and spoke. "Well heeded
is well heard." But I did not answer, I went on speaking
to Teacher Brown, asking him who was down here with him
in hell's hot sands, from manor-born to just commerown.
He said, "It is good to know about some deads down here
on this walk with me; about the rest of them, let them be.
For our time is too short to engage in idle pointless talk.
Long story short: We were all professionals of true worth,
men and women of letters, scholars of high renown all
brought down by arrogance and excess love of self.
I would tell you more but now I see some fresh steam
rising out of the sand, and some parvenu duppies I want
to avoid are at hand. Hear what I say, don't cry for me or
pity me. Read my books, they vindicate me. In my words
I am alive and I am no duppy." So saying he turned sprinting
across that fiery plain like a runner competing in a race,
and then he seemed like one who ran ahead and passed
the tape first and not as one who had come in dead last.

– from Dante's *Inferno*, Canto XV

TO THE HEIRS OF LOW BEQUESTS TO HARVEST AND
GLEAN ABUNDANT SECTIONS OF FAVELAS AND DUNGLES
WHOSE EVENING FIRES RISE GEHENNA-LIKE
FROM CITIES OF WASTE WILLED AS ESTATE
AND INHERITANCE BY SCAVENGER FOREPARENTS

Because boundaries are in dispute and vultures
draw coal-winged territorial imperative
claiming discoverer status,

the harvesters become wingless predators
with hawk's eyes and cast-iron stomach
of carrion-feasting birds.

They develop internal divining rod and compass
to isolate, assess and detect various degrees
of decomposition,

make rank savoury stew from condemned carcasses
providing the rot has not completely invaded,
penetrated through

to marrow bone, the centre free from corruption.
They feast on unstamped meat, convert the poisons
by the grace of need.

"God of outcasts we ask that you bless this trickle down
repast, sanctify the what-left this day has provided."

The fabulous sequined brassiere of a rhumba dancer
(in memoriam Margarita) graces an old woman's head,
bright-horned valkyrie crown.

She strides, ragbag diva, across her elevated garbage
stage, attendant child trails lace camisole of ex-beauty
queen's evening gown.

Dungle children at play prize bent, twisted chassis
of wrecked automobiles and broken bicycles. They ride
reckless, abandoned

along beaten down paths, ragged pennants of jeng-jeng
stream from aerials which no longer receive or send
direct messages.

From crashed car dashboards severed refrains
drip, scores are trapped behind jammed signal bands
of still radios.

Favela and dungle dwellers, children of nothing new
cherish so the mother moon when her full face
brims to overflow

and illuminates by-night excavations. They dig deep
then for items which gleam, washed-over-gold,
semi-precious gemstones,

in hope of finding one or two smooth silver spoons
fallen careless from the mouths of deposed kings,
or a lost, cast-off, golden ring.

FOR LOVE OF MARPESSA DAWN

Long summer vacation 1963.
After seeing *Black Orpheus*
Garth Baker confessed his love
for the gorgeous Marpessa Dawn.

He had been going to Cross Roads
to see her at the State Theatre
and after some seven matinees
and two or so midnight shows

he was convinced that she
was his destiny. As soon as he
finished sixth form he was going
to take a banana boat to Brazil.

Once there, he'd slip past Cerberus
in the form of a massive-headed
wharf dog and find his way to Rio
to meet Marpessa outside a theatre.

There he would serenade her
upon a lute, lyre, or box guitar
with a slow ska, a hard rocksteady,
a sweetie-come-brush-me bossa nova

till she recognized him as Orpheus
returned from the underworld.

And we believed him. We were
willing to make that leap of faith

for we were all misplaced beings,
our true selves ripped from the world book
of myths. But Garth had found his identity
and he would be reunited with Eurydice,

one radiant Marpessa Dawn.

ROMANY SONG

Where is the man who said you looked like a gypsy,
whose hands roamed the dark thicket of your hair
whispering how your hoop earrings were Romany?

Here's to the gypsy man, himself long disappeared,
to whom you brought good fortune, crossing his palm
with silver proceeds from your mendicant years.

Ai Gypsy, they burnt you too along with the Jews,
for your deep eyes which could see too far,
your loose leggobeast way, your unschooled song.

Manitas de Plata, hands of silver pluck and draw
India and Egypt through the strings of a guitar,
Gypsy Kings of the unhemmed fevered singing.

And the strum vibrato of song that will not settle
into being contained, tamed with a ring in its nose,
led to safe place to become becalmed, settled down.

Gypsy man wanders, son of Camargue horse breeders
tinkers at broken down motor cars, makes them run
like fiery chariot-wagons over shifting horizon.

Siberian winds
held him hard
up against the east wall
but rudeboy broke free,
ripped off Joseph's coat
and rode west.
You're in the aisle seat
every seam leaking
dark light. Granite love
urging you to drink from
the crystal skull
sacrificial bowl.
But your refusal to imbibe
is another rhyme.
This was Miles.
Prince of horn come to charm
you out of yoke and bit.
Kind of Blue, Time After Time
he piped till all your strained
seams split and let fall
long water, vital heartwash.

THE GARDEN OF ST. MICHAEL IN
THE SEVEN-HILLED CITY OF BAMBERG

I believe St. Michael to be my friend. He the broadsword
wielding warrior commander and captain of the righteous
host and army. I saw him once in profile, just a glimpse,
limned in the pitch dark of the stone garden where the mad
serpent-heart bull-body was trying hard to swallow me.

In the name of "woman no cry" St. Michael manifested
and trashed him like a common pickpocket. But he asked
me never again to speak of it. Nor of all his other victories
angelic and chivalric. I intend to keep these acts secret.
He's asked me to tell you instead about his garden.

For that is what St. Michael does, he gardens to unwind
from vanquishing the host of the global bad mind.
He has drawn up a plan on the ceiling of his chapel
in the seven-hilled city of Bamberg, chosen plants
he has admitted into the garden flourishing in heaven.

In the cultivated beds grow the lavender, the evergreen,
lilies arum, of the valley and white, gentians, cowslips,
Turk's head cactus and mint, camomile and castor oil,
foodkind in the garden aye pregnant pumpkins, pears, apples,
tomatoes and corn, cleansing aloes for cathartic purposes,

and tobacco to calm. Here I'm asking him to consider
a sunny corner of his garden for a few plants Jamaican

like the sansivira or donkey's ear, the low-ranking
periwinkle, aka ram-goat-dash-along, because the Christ
rode upon a donkey to go and become holy scapegoat.

And because it is written how the poor, the contrite
and cleansed are blessed, the inclusion of poor man's
orchid, Job's tears and the cerasee would seem to be
fitting, in-order and completely appropriate. And good
saint gardener Michael, let there be roses upon roses.

I AM WEARY OF ALL WINTERS MOTHER

I fear I will stop strangers
in the snowbanked street
to confide "my mother is dead."

By Borders on Ash Wednesday
a white-haired woman wears
an ash cross on her forehead.

I am weary of all winters mother,
winter within, winter without
strict-fast Ramadan, Lenten do-without.

The blessed Jessye Norman at morning
the keening Kathleen Battle each night

that is how she endures the ice age
with its freezings, exactness, deferrals.

January to May, regular doses of spirituals.
And Heathcliff has been sending her messages

scripted in code on cedar chips. Sharp cedar
scent of his cologne, cedar, the tree of coffins.

Can you not see she is dying in this winter
while you work away and send messages?

Here she is wearing a long hot-pink dress
with a floating sheer fringed black scarf.

She has bought and paid for carioca shoes,
all her long legs want to do now is dance;

and present, attentive, Heathcliff knows this.
Coffin biter has been sending her messages,

maps marked with the best place for trysts
and costly night show tickets to the Follies.

POOR MRS. LOT

And so it was that Lot's hard-ears wife
became a pillar of solid eye water.

Poor woman, frozen there crystalline
up from ground, salt stalagmite.

One last glance at what you left behind:
your mother's cutlery, your yellow plates.

One more look behind to memorize
the lay, the order of the landscape.

The red water tank. The church spire.
One last look is enough to petrify.

Like you, she should have cried
as she left, not daring to look back,

savouring hard homeground with salt.

POMO'S HYMN

Through cities of glass
the edge penitents go

pierced thinskinned parts
veiled in widow clothes.

Devotees of the order
of St. Ironheart

stigmata studded
with hard rock metal

utter urban glossolalia
exalt pure void at centre.

Through capitals of murder
the silent seraphs wing

shifting bodies from beneath
rushing oncoming wheels

emptying crack venomcups
refilling same with cerasee tea

so a one unknowingly
ingests good bitter not bad

so compunctionless is balmed
by the unctions of the band

intervening unseen
the passing winged.

HOW SHE CAME TO LEAVE AFRICA

When the tribe elected her praise singer
you started encouraging her to go,
to drop guano words how time had come
for some to leave the ancestral house,
to suggest there could be no adequate
recompense for rendered services.

That she should try her luck abroad,
become chattel hut dweller and suck salt
while you became chief and grew large,
for a continent would not be big enough
for you all. Besides she owed her luck
and election to sangoma status to you.

Hence she would forever be in your debt
with such interest not even the IMF
would charge. Big chief, can you not recall
her years of faithful service to the tribe
as light-under-bushel,
ashy foot attendant,
kitchen bitch,
live-in-maid,
grass weeder,
domestic helper,
Cookie, Nanny,
servant gal and school girl,
fool fool Rose

afflicted with tsetse fly bite, timbim,
riverblindness, chronic falling down,
leeches and sleeping sickness.
She who gave you reason to sound click
and pronounce "poor you, poor you meet it."

Sell her out sell her quick
for fast money to the first coffle
passing through the village.
Sell her while she sleeps the sleep
induced by the stale tainted palm wine
from the husk cup of false make-up.

Sell her out because a continent
was not deep or wide enough.
Thus she landed in Xamayca stricken
with quest fever, orphaned,
of no state or people and no map
to find her way back except verse.

You are born so, you know.
You can't really buy this thing.
How to explain how one day
you just wake and hear unseen voice
dictating holy and transcendent things
and your pen and heart just start decoding.

At first she would hide the evidence
made manifest at puberty,
a bright birthmark

like a faceted gemstone
glowing on her left knee,
and after that the secrets
of the trade and stones
became known to her,
goods/slaves/sugar
treetears/self-heal/amber.

Some days she would wake
to find messages inscribed
across her palms.
She could not read then
so she washed her hands
and drank the water.
And over one hundred million
words were committed
to memory, and interior
in this way too she learned
the code of colour.

Courage is the dyestuff
of the tawny lion's pelt,
bloodbath
the raw waters of the Atlantic
bearing from birth Continent.

One branch of the Nile river
is the foam shade of salt,
open sores
of slavery

and apartheid cry
for gold sulphur
reparations bath.

A fresh cut
severed heart string
bleeds liquid bronze
like molten masks of Benin.

From shameports
we passed through
whale-belly nights
of no return
and the tears
of forced parting
were the translucence
and hue
of a chalkfaced
waning yam harvest moon.

Before she learned
the names of birds,
all save the blacksmith plover
which mates for life
and dings a ringing cry
like hammer upon anvil
attacking high elephants
in defense of its young,
before she learned bird science,
they sold her, they bought her,
and she was gone.

NATAL SONG

I come to find my vital self left back here
so that I land in Xamayca with quest fever
and all the while Africa you had my remedy,
my baraka in your mouth, so that even
when they split and redirected your course
my name remained a seed under your tongue.

Khakibos and lantana spray us with green
shrapnel as we plunge through the Natal bush
this Sunday in search of the sleeping rhino.
Rendra riding shotgun displays a mandala
drawn for him by the wild Tuareg, Awad,
a black ink seal against Indonesian dungeons.

We debate upon the possible effectiveness
of a paper charm to ward off Suharto,
then all conclude that maybe a bush bath
of khakibos might do as well since it repels
insects and possibly all crawling pestilence.
So we progress through the Sunday sleeping bush.

Near here a lion ripped life from a woman's throat,
but for us the wildebeests descend from cave walls.
They are now proceeding in an undulating charge
across the high veldt, underhides gleam through
sparse pelt hairs. Marvel that this wild woman
has lived to see the running of the wildebeests.

Buck, eland and antelope all now crouch down
under the smite of midday southern Africa sun.
An equestrian black and white striped convention
conferences beneath writhing acacia trees, and Clare
reveals how the first task of the newborn zebra calf
is to memorize its mother's unique schizoid makeup.

We call upon the elevated and figured giraffe,
its sandpaper tongue swiftly negotiating round
thorns plaited into the tender foliage at the crown
of trees, city stories high. In the high lion-coloured
grass sit two females with necks like obelisks,
horns and ears imitate intricate Nubian knots.

Continent of my foremothers, to reach back I have
crossed over seas, oceans, seven-sourced rivers.
Under my heartbeat is where you pitched and lodged
persistent memory, rhythm box with no off-switch,
my drumbeat and monitor which never let me
settle for barracoon, barracks, camp or pagoda.

The veldt resounds with the ringing hammer
upon anvil cry of the fiery blacksmith plover.
All the time source was remedy for quest fever,
for the lion at your birth straddled your sign,
sacrificed appropriate sheep and beat back dogs
designating your song as the bleat of scapegoat.

Now the pride of even stricter lion demands
the total banishment of the captured within,

the scour and disinfection of mental barracoon,
the break and burial of old iron. Nothing less.
If you rise up full grown, assent and embrace,
will lion open your throat and silence, or lionize?

Thank you God for this day most amazing. Amen
good driver Adrian. Tomorrow I will drink bush tea
on the Island of Salt, realizing that we never
did see the rhino. But the wicked toe of the ostrich
excavated a stone with the seal of a mother and child
upon it. Kenzurida found it; and Africa, I kept it.

Journal Entry:
Before dawn we land
on Ilha do Sal
the airport lounge
under a fluorescent sun
blooms orange socialist chairs
like rows of hibiscus.

Ilha do Sal. That is where for three dollars U.S.
you buy a cup of bush tea such as you'd receive
in the house of a humble Jamaican person.
You purchase too a perfume sold under the slogan
"Life is best lived without a plan."

You've watched him go under every time the waves rise.
You shout from the shore reminding him how
you are his lifeguard, mender, minder with elastoplast
arms. But he dives deeper. What to do, what a life.

You board the plane for the high veldt where hyenas
laugh at humanity, and the bush falls green in winter.
You too will howl at the moon over Africa.

You could have turned that tank around and kept going
through lion country, but you are too old for such folly.

Besides, you can only sleep if diving one is beside you.
You can lie still on a presbyterian bed narrow as the straight
road to heaven. You fit tongue and groove, dovetailed corners
of armoires. That is your way.

Don't send any more messages. The last one said
"there is a place here for you." That is a ruse.
There is no place for us, neither in lamb nor lion country.

On Ilha do Sal you buy bush tea, you leave. Live your life
perfumed with no plan. Return, ask the deep diving one
how are things in the ocean?

The goat's head lies now so still
eyelashes sealed in flyblown sleep
short bone shanks crossed at rest
splintered broken drumsticks over
basin's rim. Only its body is missing.

They are selling it in halves in another part
of Victoria's market. The goat's head is red
with wet curls, behold the obliging smile.
It lay its head on the block so sinners
could lay their sins on its back and then
in gratitude drive it into the desert

there to meekly sound a lambent goodbye
as they slit its throat and skin its hide
and stretch it seamless into a public drum.
Lion says those days are done, let each one sacrifice
themselves, let everyone now pay for their own sin.
Let there be no more sell-out of the scapegoat
in any half or part of Victoria's market.

AMANDLA

Serve notice to the mind's crouching occupant who smiles
for fear of the tyrant,

the sad minstrel singing slow because undiluted rhythm
might sound too much for them.

Banish the witch doctor and necromancer who paid
for the padlocked-lipped bullfrog

to frighten your freed spirit and seal your mouth
from bearing witness.

Pay off the required cowrie shells, beads, salt and praise
to the lame busha and bucky missis.

Never mind their feigned disappointment in you,
their "whoever heard of such independence"

when they were betting on your sure demise.
Having studied your shanks they were positive

that such legs were ideal for leaping over the side
of ships, and the naysayers had such a sweet eulogy

crafted that they were going to read for you
and look how you gone and confound all nations.

Around the core and centre,
heart of amber, essence of tiger.

Muscle into flesh, tendon onto bone,
oiled joints turn smooth together.

Inhalation of elemental thunder,
breathe out steady fixed fire.

Wild fire for strivers.
Fixed flame. Essence of tigers.

Her love identified her
with the help of a museum curator
who said, "she who is golden
with fossil chips of memory
encased in her being, is Amber,
and amber is the essence of tigers."

Be careful how you wear her
around your neck, suspended
from a long thin chain, lest she
(not realizing her full strength)
should fall, and in falling
tear at your breast.

If you would keep her
keep her claws trimmed.
Learn how the pulling action
of kisses retracts thorns
still embedded in her flesh.

In tiger country the grass grows
high (twenty five feet and over).
Knowing this they sent tall hunters
to wind her in wide bolts of muslin,
their aim being to kill and eat
every atom of her being.

Mostly though it's her heart they're after
to make red medicine of courage.
But Amber tiger would always melt
into amber, transparent fossilized resin
of evergreen. All they could find of her
were gold beads from her regenerating tree.

They ask him now, "how did you get her
to come and live domesticated with you?"
But her love does not answer.

Together they study silence,
wait for night and sleep by day,
by the light of new moons they seek
and find secret feeding sources.
This way the ringmasters have never managed
to rope them in to their sad circuses.

"How did you get her to stay?"
they insist. "What trace did you find
that the other headhunters missed?"
Her love just sits silent and smiles
and runs clean hands along her stripes.

SHINING ONE

You'd be able to tell this fellow,
he shine like new money.
                    – August Wilson

I engaged the finder man
the seller of pots and pans
to search for you for me.

I paid him good money,
sold my gold guard ring
(it was protecting nothing).

I gave finder man the proceeds
and said, "go find my shining man."
The walkabout never did return.

After centuries I settled for
a succession of mattesomeones,
but religiously when dark season

came on, I would want for shining.
To finder man, seller of pots and pans
I had given this basic description:

"Look for the one with big clean hands
and the soulcase that is transparent."

I lost my money, forfeited the fee,
the errant locator never did return.
But one day, a Sunday, in January

I sighted what appeared to be a bonfire
in my garden, for the flame of the forest,
the japanese lanterns and the candlewood

were hot ablaze and the late poinsettia
leapt like flambeaux at the gateway.
I ran downstairs in my nightgown

to investigate this garden arson
and I saw you there, lost in wonder
at my full bloom conflagration.

Shining man, radiant, let finder man
keep the money from the gold ring.
Enter, come burnish my life, my being.

TO ABSORB THE GREEN

To endure the strict days of ice and winter
come absorb the green of December grass
that the egrets bring. Silk cotton blossoming.

Sunday morning waters reflect lozenge light
and dark green foliage; a thousand leaf nuances.
Do not leave Xamayca forever, your wild self

sprouts here like long-limbed guinea grass
dispersed, blown about and tossed, seeded first
off the Guinea Coast. You are African star grass.

Settle lightly, moved by breath of unknowing.
The egrets perch upon the trees like birds,
blossoms of birds, or white-feathered flowers.

MEDICINE BUNDLE OF A BLACKFOOT WOMAN

If this medicine bundle tends to remind you
of a delicacy duckonoo, a tie-leaf parcel wrapped
in banana leaf or trash,

know that it contains more than cornmeal
or red-skinned potato sweet and steamed.
It holds within cures,

the stuff of dreams and antidotes for ridding
you of the effects of evil eye. I have been
making it for years.

A medicine woman of the Blackfoot Nation
told me how to start it with a root shaped
like a clean heart.

She told me to bundle it and pray sincerely
for goodness, kindness, and mercy to follow
me. In time I added

such things I found as I trod through earth,
things to heal the effects of slip and fall down.
Righteous rosemary,

the navel string of my son, my mother's last look
(she looked like a bride), her countenance washed
and clarified

the essence of sincerity and hard-to-cultivate
forgiveness. How can that hold in it you ask?
And I say don't worry about it.

It's my medicine bundle, don't it?

OUTWAITING THE CRAZY WOLF MOON

In the North country the native people
call this the moon when wolves go crazy.
Here, they warn against gathering grass wiss
and bamboo at the time of the full moon's rising.

For that is when the chi-chi larvae swarm
in bamboo joints and wiss is alive with insects.
You will find that what you have gathered
is a bundle of useless sticks, sick with parasites.

It is wise to wait for the timely rise
of the verdigris moon called "glad to be alive."
Soon after will follow the one of new life,
the moon of pure silver which presides over

the melting of the ice, the earth as it thaws
and causes resurrection lilies to appear
defiant by hard walls of penitentiaries,
burst out sudden from cracks in tombs

and bloom in the yards of faithful lovers
who bit their tongues and sucked salt
as they learned strict patience and outwaited
the mad moon of the crazy wolves.

After, her body became a container for stars.
Some nights when the room would go dark
she would feel the movement of the sun's cars
burning her bare soles with traction marks,
racing upwards on the red rush of her blood
via capillaries arteries and veins till they emerged
from her rib cage and triumphantly parked
beside the hunter with his jewelled girdle
and his dog, guarding the live ruby of her heart.
Outside her, the three sisters and pilot moons
would be braiding her hair and anointing her feet,
and what others took for wind-zephyring tunes
was really the call and response of the Pleiades
singing sweet constellations in her sleep.

THE ROSE CONFLAGRATION

Last night that gift of roses
just combusted into flames
after I shut the blue door
and recited your names.

If those without ever imagined
that the artist of Murray Mountain
had painted a hill landscape
that caused a rose conflagration,

the inflaming of a rose fire
in this small rented space . . .
But anyway, I was telling you
that those blooms of rose-peach

that blushed red at the edges
of the petals burst into a bouquet
of bright flames, roseate candles
this post advent ember day.

And I witnessed the exact moment
that these holy roses ignited
and bloomed torch and open
because your names were recited.

STUDIO I
BROTHER EVERALD BROWN

An elder, an artist, a Rastafarian
who dwells upon Murray Mountain
St. Ann, where springs the lambs' bread
colly. He paints the dreamscapes alive
behind his locks, Ethiopian Coptic scenery,
multiple mountains and fallow clouds
inclined to rain down angels. Sometimes
he shapes pregnant-bellied instruments
which breed cosmic sounds for Egyptian
winds to zither across their strings.

STUDIO II
SEYMOUR L.

The winter after she left him
he made pictures of flying women,
line drawings of long-tressed
lithe comely women in flight
often heading over the Hudson
leaving just their trunks and legs
to remain in the composition.
Some faceless ones would enter
head first into the chaste square
of Arches paper. Half in half out,
constructed to always be without
his complete vision and framing.

STUDIO III
PETRONA MORRISON

rises early and raises tall shrines
fills clay cups with spirit palm wine
salvages the remains of charred cities
and rests them on beds of fragrant leaves.
Bring the symbols of hard life come,
bring the gunmetal, barbwire and bomb
and watch her bend them into shapes
which encircle and reconnect.

STUDIO IV
BARRINGTON WATSON

There is a woman lying on a bed
spread with zinc white sheets,
a boychild on a chamberpot throne
in a twilight room.
The countenance of the boy
is that of a child well fed
on slow-boiled cornmeal porridge
which luminizes the skin.
The woman looks pensive.
Outside the canvas stands
another son, a master
who immortalized
his own dark mother
with a nod to Whistler.

CÉZANNE AFTER ÉMILE ZOLA

Émile, your friend from childhood
turned his pen and drew your blood,
created a character with your features
and cast him as an artist manqué
of coarse peasant's dress and rude speech,
a suicide with no sugar for his morning tea
whose vision was crazy, cracked impasto.

When they belittled you, the them
who in the end do not count or matter,
your blood ran choleric. What camp follower
can ever see far? But when Émile
cut you so, your blood became acid, vitriol,
green gall. Solitary you painted Mont Sainte-Victoire
over and over until you drew and coloured
a hard mountain range for a heart.

The sky breaks in unblended strokes,
the stones in your landscapes separate.
The features of the perpetual bathers
become gross. Constantly you wash
the memorystain of first friendship
before Zola's achievement in Paris.
Over and over you recreate boy's memory
of friendship carried by clean streams.

The accidental brush
of a serving maid's sleeve,
your son's small hand
as you crossed a street,
the presence of your woman.
After Zola, you could not stand
the touch of them or most humans.

WHEN THEY TOOK DOWN THE SUN OF TABRIZ

When they stabbed at Shams
with their envy knives

they pierced absence,
steel rent just garments.

There fell two drops of blood,
more red sweat put forth

in final Darwish effort
to rise with Jesus

and Mohammed
into the empyrean.

Shams had reintegrated
with The Beloved

and Rumi keened
requiem high dirges

threnodies of the separated
ripped from wild reed bed.

Egypt being the home of embalmers, you gaze
at the perfectly kept and laid out under preservation spices.
The shrine to remember is that of the poet Sakinah,
located down a side alley with boys at play outside
tended by an old woman with kohl-rimmed eyes
who sweeps and dusts, so the shrine is clean enough
to pass the inspection of any house-proud poet saint.
The shrine keeper's ancient countenance pearls.
St. Sakinah is at rest in her glass chamber in lavish
lace-edged robes and somehow you think she knows,
that she can hear the petition you are weary of asking
for the Paraclete to draw near and bring assuaging
to deflect the strong interference and dull stabbing
in your heart. "If you ask her to pray for you, you will be
relieved of your sadness" says Ali, and you asked.

SONG FOR THOMAS MERTON

The Beloved called you and whispered the secret
close to that great heart, then bid you speak it.

Sift chaff from wheat, obfuscation from truth,
then convert high wisdom into plain food.

Swallow the whole silence of the blue Kentucky air
till loves peals out clear so, Brother Louis cantor.

Feed upon said silence and become still and sated.
Devotees stood outside the walls of Gethsemane

and waited to see the high smoke signal rise
from the alchemical fire of your hermitage.

You stand in Papine market three years to the day of your
    mother's death

and marvel at the sight of fifty-seven bottles of coconut oil
    gleaming, longnecked,

and count as many of St. Thomas logwood honey, making you
    want to chant "Glory"

for the sight of earth bounty, blessed be the green country
    yielding this food.

Weight of ground provision, cornucopia of fruit. Sugarloaf
    pineapple old lady sells,

says the small hole in it was drilled by woodpecker's beak
    because mango season finish.

Of the hole too in heart-fruit, drilled long, drilled deep, how
    come some seed time

and lie-fallow last so long? Why some water diligently and is
    chaff they reap?

You don't know the answer, just sing slow and hold to the
   rosewater flesh of naseberry,

chant OM like bees in logwood thicket, blessing selling in the
   market.

CROSSOVER GRIOT

The jump-ship Irishman
who took that Guinea girl
would croon when rum
anointed his tongue.

And she left to mind
first mulatta child
would go end of day
to ululate by the bay.

"I am O'Rahilly" he croons.
She moans "since them
carry me from Guinea
me can't go home"

Of crossover griot
they want to ask
how all this come about?
To no known answer.

Still they ask her
why you chant so?
And why she turn poet
not even she know.

LEANNA

Great grandmother Leanna I approach
your roadside house at Kendal Westmoreland
bringing moneygifts and word from Doris

my mother who says to tell the old man
Francisco, your grandson born in Cuba
travelling now in the front room

with the wire cage of turtle doves
warbling him home, that should he cross over
soon, he must tell the generations

that Dear Dor and Dear Ann, the only ones
left, are holding on. Though the stretched
enlarged labouring heart in Doris's case

and the trapped ice in Ann's joints
cause them to move slow, they hold.

They are from your line Leanna,
long-lived line of Guinea women.
It's your strong scent I've identified,

your cinnamon escallion essence
burning on my eyelids when subway cars
stop without warning inside dark tunnels.

The small gust that cools my heels
when I'm inclined to turn sharp down
one-way streets is the scrape of your crêpe soles

bought white and dyed black
to distinguish them from "dem lil gal."

In extreme cases you have mounted
your wide flanked grey mule and trampled
underhoof the spoiling plans of the ones

who think that because I'm an orphan
I have no one. Make them go on.

I approach your roadside house Leanna,
lift nets of lovebush from your tomb
and bear my mother's message
to the traveller in the front room.

SISTER ROSITA

sifts through the cast off clothes
for the poor, to one side she folds
the stale garments society ladies
will not wear again, those they donate
to the less fortunate, dresses stained
with banquet sauce and wine.

Her eyes slide past the day wear,
the pastel and muted shades
of matrons, until she spots
a disturbance of a red dress, flash
of gold trim, a blouse writhing
paisley print or dyed in boldface
African violet ink.

In her cell without mirrors
she feels the red fabric
inflame her hips, its sizing
crisp her nipples. She drapes
the gold scarf in a secular stole
and waltzes to chimes of earlier bells
before the morning hour of primes.

PETITION TO THE MAGDALEN

I

Eight days before my birthday is when
they celebrate your saint's day.
Did you ever see the four candles
I lit in your high church
in Toronto one winter?

You never speak to me.
I have never seen you in a dream
except for my Egyptian alabaster jar
which I like to think contained
spikenard for anointment

and my great capacity
for weeping maundy tears
enough to wash face, hands and feet.
You never associate with me
who, like you, wasted my love so

while waiting for the one
who could tell me all I ever did.
But you never speak to me,
Magdalena, even when I went
to the desert and lived in your cave.

You only left messages,
cryptic petroglyphs, but one day
you caused my shadow self to separate
from me, took me from behind myself
like Augustine.

I never met him at the well.
Perhaps it would take too long to tell
all that I ever did.
It was my heart he went after,
took it from my chest
while I slept late and careless,
washed it in well water,
woke and ordered me
to the desert to wander.

Gave me a water song to sing
even as I wandered thirsting
with you as my absent patron saint.

Alabaster jar for anointing.
Costly spikenard.
Capacity for tears enough
to wash feet
hands and hearts.

I came after you to the tomb
but He was already gone.
Magdalena will you come
to me

now that my mother
can make for me
on spot intercession?
And did you
accept the four
candle flames,

indulgences I purchased
for my son my mother
my true friend and me?
And could you just appear
now, saint of wild women,
in a dream?

II

Magdalena,
you know that story
the one where Jesus
did not ascend into heaven
but survived crucifixion
and you and he settled down
and raised children?

I doubt its veracity.
Let's face it Magdalena,
some women are not the kind
that men marry.

They are love's substitute nurses
who draw venom
from men's veins,
and swab and stitch
eviscerated egos.

Manpride thrown down
in soiled laundry,
they refresh in the well
of Samaritan ministry.

That the son of man
honoured you is a good story,
that he knew all you ever did

but loved you still,
that he considered himself
blessed to take
a woman experienced as wife.

A woman tender and capable
of washing his feet with her tears,
of drying them with her hair,
of bearing it out beyond doom,
of arriving there before
the Easter sunrise to balm
his murdered self with spices.

The sisters of your first order
are working still,
The piece of papyrus
detailing the end
of your story is lost.
But Magdalena, loyal follower,
"dear friend," what was the true end
of your story?

IRON SHIRT

I'm gonna put on a iron shirt
and chase satan out of earth.
— Maxie Romeo

Respect due to the man who would chant
that song. The same man wandered
about the hot streets of Kingston
wearing nothing but a gash red wound,
open wound he received when Shaitan
took molten scissors to his iron shirt,
cut his well-intentioned armour off
and told the third world knight
to take a walk.

It is 3 a.m. You wake from beside
your beloved who rode through snows
to join you. You loved so, then lay down
to sleep and that is when goddamned Shaitan
comes in through dream gates to seed
fear images.

Beneficent watchman who never sleeps,
see how this freezing night has driven
duppy and daemons indoors to leech
on light and lovespirit. Cold-blooded
creatures, spirit tramps want now
to burn bad lamps.

There is no place here for them to pitch
these malevolent leather-winged spirits.
Not here, not now.
Watchman, drive all wretched
from this house.

MY ISLAND LIKE A SWIMMING TURTLE

My island like
a swimming turtle
surfaces in the fishtank
of the television

black rubber tire smoke
belching from its breath
and machete chops
and gunshots on its carapace.

We suck our turtle children
unformed out of our eggs
and boil and boil ourselves
in vicious mannish water.

Our bigman fat posse
eat beef Wellington
even on Ben Johnson day.
Feastdays, we suck salt.

War correspondents
come with seeing eye
cameras to show dirty
turtle laundry to the world,

how our big sea fishermen
cannot swim.

Cry out O terrapin.

ST. THOMAS

St. Thomas Aquinas, doctor of the church, determined
from he was a small boy to go and serve his master
and not even his mother, his siblings who held him
captive at Rocca Secca could stop him.

Is the good doctor name saint of Deacon Bogle's birthplace?
Did St. Thomas walk with Paul Bogle when he journeyed,
determined to bring the hard news of black people's suffering
to Eyre, he of the stone heart?

From Stony Gut past the bile yellow Yallahs River
through the valley of decision to the colonial square
did the good doctor walk the long way with our Paul?

Summa Theologica, did he counsel, instruct and reassure
him that he too was always from birth, determined?
Was he there when they hanged him? Should not this Parish
and place now be called St. Thomas St. Paul?

ST. CATHERINE

She moves among the fallen in the district prison,
St. Catherine who from early took the way
of the desert saints, occupiers of small cells,
making unending intercession for the broken world.

St. Catherine walks with them to the tower of the hangman.
St. Catherine chants change into hearts of sleeping felons.
St. Catherine watches over the innocent fallen among them,
appoints contrite murderers to protect defenceless young men.

Forgive now the lapses and errors which lead to early hell.
St. Catherine knows hard labour. Her family sentenced her
to domestic imprisonment for the crime of taking orders
from above. To banish her propensity for visions she was made

to scrub stone floors, bake coarse bread and cultivate grudging
ungrateful gardens. Her roomcell became a paradise of lights
and sweet, ecstatic consolations never known by worldlians.
St. Catherine intercedes for the lost, the thieves, the dog hearts,

violators wicked and most fallen. She writes letters of intercession
to Queens, Prime Ministers and Governors General, tells her long
rosary along Monk Street each morning, and walks to the gallows
with the violent and condemned who lose their heads.

ST. MARY

The sea leaps like the baptizer child in your cousin's womb
when she saw you. The heart rises up too at the sight
of Port Maria in the parish of St. Mary. The Caribbean sea
the exact colour and shade of your dress, blue, inspired
painters catch and blend from cobalt, lapis, the sea itself.
St. Mary mother of all babies, parishes and entire countries,

you whom the by-the-book married mothers' union
would not have allowed into the daughters of the king.
Patron Saint of this corner of rock-of-my-heart, Xamayca
here and ninety miles away little girls named Mary, Maria
Innocente, and Maria Concepción sell their small selves
for small gain.

Across the Caribbean tonight the motherless
are rocked by belching soundboxes prophesying
their future, death by guns and milk-white cocaine.
A new Code Noir is across the region good mother.
The hope of the small must be buried at night
in a remote potters' field in an unmarked grave.

The sea turns like the drape and folds of your dress.
Do you know what they do in your name?

QUESTIONS FOR MARCUS MOSIAH GARVEY

And did prophets ascended come swift
to attend you at the end
in your small cold water room in London?

Was it William Blake now seraph and ferryman
who rowed you across the Thames to where Africans
took you by longboat home?

And did the Nazarene walking upon water
come alongside to bless and assure you that he
of all prophets understood and knew

just how they had betrayed and ill-used you?
And did you wonder again what manner of people
sell out prophets for silver and food?

LUSH

Perhaps if you remain you will become civilized,
detached, refined, your words pruned of lush.
Lush is an indictment in this lean place
where all things thin are judged best.
What to do then with the bush and jungle
sprouting from your pen?

The dream house at Enfield where you received
poet's schooling. House with slightly cultivated garden
bearing black-eye and congo peas beside English roses.
Loose curled heads of lettuce sheltered under yam hills,
red-pulp oxheart tomato tethered to quicksticks
of unhemmed tearaway fence

round the yard's swing-skirt circumference.
Japanese lanterns threatening to raze coffin wood
of tall rank cedar tree. And beneath it a running
river babbling deep water glossolalia in spate,
summoning the shy river mumma to appear.
By a full moon you can read by, she would coil

her fish half on a smooth rock, and comb and
comb her long water-wave hair. Cain and Abel
lived in the village. When Abel was slaughtered
Miss Jamaica paraded his head on a sceptre
as she rode in her win-at-all costs motorcade.
From his blood sprung a sharp reproach bush

which drops karma fruit upon sleeping policemen
to remind them of their grease-palm sins of omission.
A bordello replaced a butchershop in the tidy square
and St. Martin de Porres became the village Patron Saint.
I could go on, but I won't. My point is finished, made.
May lush remain the way of my world.

BAM CHI CHI LALA

It is fall again, October rains
and red trees signal you
are entering change season.
Your guinea blood courses fierce
and you think to drink gold leaf
in a camel bid to store sun.
See how your small boy
has become a fine man.

You cross the street to bless brides
and cross yourself as ambulances shriek by.
This morning you woke at five and kept
company with the monk of Gethsemane,
lauds and aubades. In Hanover your people's
river swells because the hurricanes
have wept and flashed their epileptic
selves across the West Indies.

How do wild spirits gain entrance
into humans?
Do they make their way through body
orifices as we sleep?
If that is so then it is best to say
the sealing prayer before slumber.
"Lord, please keep all demons away
from the nine gates of my body."

Or better still, forsake shuteye,
join the night watch and patrol
the border country between
the worlds of sleep and wake.

Do small deeds of love for the world.
Remove traps and tripping stones
set by the wicked for the weak.
With the aid of clean mirrors
bring the lost from behind themselves.
And then pass silent by graveyards
taverns and public cotton trees where
the ambitious hold duppy conventions.

Aye, earth's garments wear so heavy.
See how much the queen's robe sags,
trimmed as it is with feathers of the vain,
sleek ermine and jewels of bright ambition.
Be wary miss monarch of the ones who come
ostensibly to admire the intricate inlaid
workmanship of your throne, for they
may be measuring your neck's length like

Queen Mary the pretender, whom some
toasted with wine glass on top of glass of water
because they said the real monarch lived over
the ocean. No one crowned her that is true,
she is a pretender just like you, save for this
one thing. The first word
you read spelled your vocation, Singer.

If they knew how all ambition
should come to this, autonomy
autonomy over the me myself.
Sovereign over self kingdom
feel free whomsoever to fight over
the cold food Babylon has left over.
Bam chi chi lala
angels dance rocksteady
on the head of a common pin.

Softly now
our Beloved
is convening
pleasant Sunday evening.

ACKNOWLEDGEMENTS

Maximum respect to Philip Sherlock, Elder. Thanks to
Veronica Gregg, Bob Weisbuch, and Tish O'Dowd of the
University of Michigan, U.S.A.; Maura Dooley of South Bank
Centre, London, England; Millicent Daley of Cambridge
College, Massachusetts, U.S.; Adriaan Donker of Poetry
Africa, Durban, South Africa; Wolf Peter Schnetz of the
Bureau of Culture, Erlangen, Germany; Reid and Jane Rubin,
and the staff at RISM, New York, U.S.A.; Tatjana Daan and
Erik Menkveld of Poetry International, Rotterdam, the
Netherlands; Lowell Fiet of the University of Puerto Rico, San
Juan, Puerto Rico; Magda Smith of the Humanities Council,
U.S. Virgin Islands; Hazel Simmonds-MacDonald of Cave
Hill Campus, Barbados, West Indies; Jean Smith of the Office
of the Vice Chancellor and Edward Baugh of Mona Campus,
Jamaica, West Indies; the blessed Professor Michael Cooke of
Yale University, U.S.A.; Sandra Pacquet and Zack Bowen of
the University of Miami, U.S.A.; Abiola Irele of Ohio State
University, U.S.A.; and Reverend Carol and Bryan Finlay of
Toronto, Canada.